FIND
THE
SILLY
ANIMALS!

There are animals to find,
SILLY as can be...
Have a look around, then point
when you see!

CAN YOU SPOT THE SILLY COWS?

CAN YOU FIND
THE SILLY LIONS?

CAN YOU SPOT THE SILLY PIGS?

CAN YOU FIND
THE SILLY MONKEYS?

CAN YOU SPOT
THE SiLLY PARROTS?

CAN YOU FIND
THE SILLY ELEPHANTS?

CAN YOU SPOT
THE SiLLY REiNDEERS?

CAN YOU FIND
THE SILLY TIGERS?

CAN YOU SPOT THE SiLLY CATS?

CAN YOU FIND
THE SILLY FOXES?

CAN YOU SPOT
THE SiLLY HORSES?

CAN YOU FIND
THE SILLY GIRAFFES?

CAN YOU SPOT THE SILLY BEARS?

CAN YOU FIND
THE SILLY SHEEP?

WELL DONE!

You've found the silly animals i see...

...and here they all are, gathered under a tree!

THE END!

Find us on Amazon!

Discover all of the titles available in our store; including these below...